GRAY LIGHTFOOT'S POETRY ON MI BUS

A collection of poems
inspired by driving buses
in Cornwall

All the best

Gray Lightfoot

1

Also by Gray Lightfoot

A View from a Cab (the poetry and musings of a bus driver in Cornwall)

The Malthouse Falcon
(the first Humphrey Boggart novel)
Bigg's Leap
(the second Humphrey Boggart novel)

Check out Gray Lightfoot's poetry at
www.graylightfoot.co.uk

Illustrations within the text are attributed to the author as no-one else wishes to claim them

INTRODUCTION

On the 22nd May 2021, I retired from bus driving. I had not been driving buses all my life like some of my colleagues, I came into it in my fifties when I moved down to Cornwall. I needed a job and not many people were prepared to offer one despite my apparent genius and self-belief. Let's say that *First Bus* were desperate...just like every other bus company...they are always on the lookout for drivers...they need to replace me for a start.

After the initial shock of driving these huge monsters around the tight lanes of Cornwall, I finally began to enjoy bus driving. Passengers...I could take or leave...but driving a bus is much more fun when you're all on your own. There is a reason for the bus drivers' mantra - "an empty bus is a happy one". Of course, there would be no point to bus driving without passengers and all bus drivers will tell you that 999.99% of them are fine...but the other .01% can really ruin your day.

I will ever be grateful to *First Bus* for taking me on (and please take note that none of the opinions in this book are that company's) because driving buses turned me back to writing poetry again. It always seems a surprise to people that driving a bus and addressing the muse could ever go hand in hand but I would say that bus driving is the perfect job for writing poetry. Most of the driving you do on autopilot (except for the open-top route where you have to concentrate for the whole fifty-one miles), where you can toss ideas around in your head on one level while you safely drive a twelve-ton bus plus passengers around the roads on another. When you arrive at your destination, if you have time, you can even write down your brilliant thoughts. Driving buses also gave me a *unique selling point* and I managed to sell quite a few copies of *A View from a Cab* (even sold a lot of them on the Mousehole bus itself). Some of the poems in that book are also to be found in this collection.

As I am no longer a bus driver, I cannot claim to be 'the bus driver poet' anymore, so I thought it would be nice to collect together all my bus driving poems in one handy book for your delectation and further enlightenment. I do hope you enjoy them as much as I enjoyed writing them.

The poet formerly known as 'bus driver'

Gray Lightfoot
May 2022

THE CORNISH BUS DRIVER'S PRAYER

Our Father, who art in Helston,
Gunwalloe be thy name.
Thy Camborne come, Newmill be done
In St Erth as it is in St Levan.
Give us St Day our daily Breage
And forgive us our Malpasses
As we forgive those who Malpas against us
And lead us not into Trengwainton
But deliver us from Eden
For thine is the Kingsley Village
The Par and the Cury
For Devoran ever
Lands End.

This poem was inspired by the apocryphal poem *The Bus Driver's Prayer* that was recorded by Ian Dury (Dury's father was a bus driver) in which the words of the Lord's Prayer were replaced by placenames on London bus routes. My poem, which started out as *The West Cornwall's Bus Drivers' Prayer* and was a challenge to find similar place names in Cornwall that fit into the prayer, has gone through a number of changes as 'better' rhyming places have been found and I have tried to give the poem a wider Cornish appeal.

A VIEW FROM A CAB (*BUSRUNNER*)

*"I've seen things you people wouldn't
believe…attack ships on fire off the shoulder of
Orion. I've watched C-beams glitter in the dark
near the Tannhäuser Gate. All those moments
will be lost in time…like tears…in rain."*

Roy Batty's final words before his replicant body
is switched off in the film *Bladerunner* (Ridley
Scott, 1982)

Scorched attack ships off Marazion?
I'm afraid that you've got me there mate;
But I've seen moonbeams glitter on dark
Solar panels near Butteriss Gate.

I've seen such red skies over Mounts Bay –
Whose crimson glory in the morning;
Would leave the most cautious of shepherds
To not give a toss for the warning.

I've seen people point with delight at
Their first sight of St Ives' golden tiles.
I've heard the intake of breath they make
At the point they become Kernowphiles.

I've seen a castle-topped island soar
Like some kind of Swiftian notion.
Rising out from a circle of mist;
Set fair to fly over the ocean.

7

I've seen Sennen Cove's resilience
In the face of one-hundred-foot waves;
The safe haven of its hardy homes
At those times when the sea misbehaves.

I've seen Mousehole's granite in close up,
Glistening feldspar, mica and quartz;
While squeezing a bus just like toothpaste
Out into this prettiest of ports.

I've seen a view from Penryn bridge where
A widening Carrick Roads ensures
A pleasure boat-bobbing sea – (ooh!) blue –
With myriad sunlit Koh-i-Noors.

I've seen steam hauling trains over Hayle;
Such moments when nostalgia enchants.
Gazing breathless as steam kisses sky;
I'm a railway child still in short pants.

I've seen myself pilot a *Spitfire*,
With Penzance all laid out before me.
Buzzing down over Newlyn's Chywoone Hill,
Having just returned from a foray.

I've seen (and winked) in Lamorna at
The old home of a Hollywood star.
Where would the pirate industry be
Without Bob Newton's scurrilous "Arrrr!"?

I've seen dead people placed…pedestalled.
High fived Trevithick; waved at Davy.
Saluted the brave that served and died
In the Air Force, Army and Navy.

I've seen courage each time in passing
The lifeboat station's flag at Penlee.
Those lost boys of the Solomon Browne
Who were braver than I'd ever be.

I've seen white horses charging the beach
Where Long Rock plays Cossack and Russian;
Witnessed their glory fade; watched as this
White brigade rides to its destruction.

I've seen signs and stones to make you smile –
Where a fingerpost points to Ding Dong!
Trewellard's name that doesn't quite fit
Or St Ives where the 'S's are wrong.

I've seen polytunnels that shimmer
And confound those assured of their sight.
Those sloping lakes seen from Trevenen
Are just quicksilver tricks of the light.

I've seen daffodils hosting game shows;
Clouds of golden gorse lining my way;
Crocosmia orange in splendour
And bluebell swathes set for Flora Day.

I've seen the joy of being alive
In a bay foal's exhilaration;
In dolphins dancing in Gwavas Lake
And in a starlings' murmuration.

I've seen ghost owls haunting and hunting –
Stealth bomb studies in alabaster;
A serpentine mink prowl in the sun –
A shadow in search of its caster.

I've seen igloos, penguins, polar bears
And scenes from a Bethlehem stable
Fashioned from neon for Christmas time
On the dark green of Praze-an-Beeble.

I've seen a twinkling black tiara
Set with jewels of luminous hue.
Our land that's beloved and displayed on
A cushion of the iciest blue.

I've seen engine houses all over,
Give the finger; a futile gesture.
As sunset alights upon Geevor
And a tin drum beats to lost venture.

I've seen riding out on the cliff tops
Ross Poldark searching out derring-do.
For a change, the people of Cornwall
Will gladly welcome the revenue.

I've seen in a winter-rimed mirror
The care-worn face, beset by the wind;
The country's most westerly driver
Writing rhyme on his own at Land's End.

Unlike Roy Batty in *Bladerunner*
(Nexus 6 played by Rutger Hauer);
I've taken precautions for the day
When it's me that runs out of power.

All those moments are not lost in time
Saved images that my brain compiles,
Are laid out for your perusal now
Replicate Roy! I backed up my files!

Bus Driver/Replicant – smell the oil!
Excuse me for not being subtle
It's up to us to record the view
From *Dennis Dart* or off-world shuttle.

I'm blessed that I get to see Cornwall
From the lowest tide to Carn Brea's top
But how much better my job would be
If I didn't keep having to stop!

The quote at the head of this poem is of one man's dismay (albeit, an artificially created man with a lifespan of a mere four years) that nothing in his exciting life has ever been recorded; and so "will be lost in time...like tears...in rain". Now, I know driving a bus in Cornwall is hardly *Battlestar Galactica*, but the more I saw of the beauty of Cornwall from the window of my bus, the more I felt the need to write about what I had seen, culminating in this poem.

ODE TO A CORNISH MILESTONE
(for Ian Thompson)

There's a milestone on the A30;
Out at Canonstown – all painted white
(By a kindly chap who keeps things nice);
That tells me home is almost in sight.

The words are succinct in their detail;
Hand-carved by some Cornish stone mason.
You know you're just five miles from Penzance –
That's in the direction you're facing.

It also says in another ten
Out Land's End you'll find yourself straying.
Then there's an icon called a benchmark
Which is useful when you're surveying.

It pleases me whenever I pass
For I know it's bang on the money,
Because what I see is 'Penzance Smiles'
And what looks like 'Land's End is sunny'.

I don't know if you have noticed the proliferation of recently-painted Cornish milestones that are popping up in the verges of our roads like huge snowdrops. Driving a bus meant that I came across a lot of these and it was always a delight to see a new one appear. Ian Thompson is the man for whom we have to be thankful to because he spent ten years of his life, out of the goodness of his heart, painting these milestones all over Cornwall. Considering they are hundreds of years old; they now look as good as new.

No 6
(A summer bus journey to Mousehole in 2016)

In Penzance bus station all but the sky seems
monochrome
On the floor, grey angles proliferate...dust
hardens.
The off-white canopy of stiff-peaked meringues
Offers the only shade to the antsy passengers
who
Ponder just how pushy or polite they need to be
As they crowd around the drowsy idling open top
bus.
Herring gulls whiter than sugar-free mints
Mooch among the detritus of such copious days;
Their sepia chicks attached like long lost souls
Constant in their mewling...'Are we there yet?'

Outside their rest room, hi-vizzed drivers vape
Exotic scents of Bourbon, Root Beer and Crème
de Menthe.
One drinks tea from a chipped *Portmeirion* mug
And watches the buses leave the stands one by
one
To reveal the runt of the litter...tiny and pink.
The Mousehole bus. Small and perfectly parked.

Eager to be off, like a bubble emerging from the
sea;
Climbing Market Jew Street, where to our right

The Terrace rises from threshold to rampart.
It is glorious summer in this seaside town
As locals and tourists squint in the discerning
light.
Nervous legs, ill-at-ease at venturing out
For the first time, crave the safe refuge of
Trousers they fear they will never see again.
Box fresh holiday trainers bask in new found
freedom
And pad the hard granite setts with a louche
abandon.
Hawaiian-shirted men posture and vie with
Ladies in elegant thin-strapped floral dresses
For a piece of precious Penzance pavement.
A crumpled and stained XXL *Cardin* t-shirt
(Which would have Pierre pulling out his hair)
Fails to break Humphry Davy's party mood
As he dons a seagull-shaped hat for the
hundredth time today
And bears the sun beating down on his powdered
face.
Behind him, the Italianate dome of the Market
House
Heralds our entry into the Georgian quarter.
Built with money made from mining metal
Aspiring to be a copper Sherborne or a tin Bath;
Its very mansions polished and partitioned
Are mined for investment or financial whimsy.

The bus now full as a shopping bag buzzes
Through the sun-dappled forest of Alverton;

A quarter mile of shade that brings us blinking out
Into The Princess Royal Estate, council as was.
Loved and lived in. No second homes here.
Mowers drone like worker bees either side of
The Ropewalk, where newly-tarred ropes
Were once laid out to be twined and dried.
Now it is the lawns that are drying out;
As pristine and sharply-cut as WI sandwiches.
Up and over the prospect of Lidden Hill;
Ladies and gentlemen, I present Mounts Bay,
A feature visible on any map of this isle
Where the open arms of The Lizard to the south
And the Lands End peninsula to the west offer
An embrace that just might take your breath
away.
And then down between an honour guard of
poppies,
Mercifully spared the council's spray on the
grounds
Of aesthetics, perhaps? A killer with a heart,
maybe?
They stand erect like long lost traffic light lollipops
Far from the bygone jar they were once kept in.
Lichen dried orange by the searing heat, peppers
The baking roof tiles like a dusting of paprika.
White walls and palm trees pervade in soft focus
Like tired old shop-bought slides of The Lebanon;
More Hockneyed than hackneyed as swimming
pool blue
The presumptuous sea comes forward to meet us
As full as an egg and brimming with sparkle.

Fuchsias bright with promise and hydrangeas,
(like those pink and blue liquorice allsorts, which
you either like or you don't), frame Newlyn's
green.

Look, look to the right where the town's houses
Stack up like a centenarian's birthday cards
On a myriad of granite mantelshelves.
Turn your face left to the rebuilt promenade;
A victim of the sea's great white bite
(The taste of land a temptation too far),
Now finds itself recovered and beloved by
'Life-coached' Lowry folk walking matchstalk
dogs,
Their silhouettes blue-screened against the railing
Provide a musical score for this summer time.
Into Newlyn town where the chip shop vinegar
smell
Hits you to encourage salivation as you pass.
The Seaman's Mission, now sold off, re-invented
As a place where salvation is no longer on the
menu.
See the old fisherman who clings to the rail
And sways as if he was still back out there.
He trawls now for gossip or companionship
Comforted by the smell of fish, freshly slit,
Slabbed and sold on the cold marble.
The fish market, whose grey breeze-block frieze
Acts as a cold cataract on your eye until
Its removal allows you to see once more
As you rise with the slip like a child being

Hoisted and held over a sweet shop's penny tray;
Your eyes keen to pick and choose from the vivid boats.
Below you, the old quay waits like the old man
Eager for new tales but left only with those
Of long ago, like that day back in 1620 when
The Mayflower made its last call on this land.

On past the granite bastions of the old quarry which
Hold back a high unseen lake, metres from the sea.
Buddleias point perfumed fingers at the lovely ladies
Whose quest for fitness and good health still
Allows them to smile and palm the air as we pass
To where lovingly-tended flowers embrace the sadness
That lingers over the deserted lifeboat station.
Its inside remains as it was left in 1981
When the Solomon Browne's bravest of the brave
Answered a shout but never called back themselves.
Adrift, St Clement's Island made skeletal by the high tide
Resembles some waking kraken full of hideous intent
To plunder Mousehole's harbour wall and coil
A tentacle or two around an unsuspecting tourist.
Then down we go into the granite labyrinth;
Matched only by the driver's practised chicanery.

A sharp judged left turn past a cannonball lodged
Amid the foundations of a cottage – a memento
Of the Spanish invasion of 1595.
Then a tight right onto the harbour where
The pushy tide reclaims the beach forcing
People to cats-cradle across the taut ropes
That seem to radiate from the harbour's entrance;
Where wet-suited children leap and laugh like seals
And dayglo kayaks, pressed like plastic pilchards,
Rest against the shadowed wall of the tiny beach.
A black cat, nervy as a witch's familiar flees the bus,
Which halts alongside the people-magnet railing
From which they hang like living lifebelts.
The bus bifurcates those reds of the dead and alive;
The perpetually-poppied cenotaph mirrored by
Those preserved boxes of living communication.
Yes, my chick, we are there now. Look, look…
A glance up ahead and there stands Dylan's hill.
"Raginnis is good for you!" he said and was right.
It was the whisky that was the death of him.

The three-point return when it's time to go;
Reverse hazard warnings break the reverie
(Their purpose when all is said and done)
Of those who gawp and squint in the sunshine.
The necessary exit on the wrong side of the road
As if the Spanish had never been repelled.
Skimming so close to the wall that we push

20

Doorway browsers into *The Mousehole* shop
Whether they want to or not (alas for no
commission).
The resilient rose that endures forty lashes a day
From the exiting bus as punishment for daring
To encroach into that jigsaw-tight space
That only just allows the bus to leave.
Up and out and once more gazing at the flat blue
Which picks out the orange of a resting tanker
Or maybe the scalloping show of a pod of
dolphins;*
A yellow trawler heading home, pinpointed by its
wake.
The breath in me expelled, a large liberating
bubble
That rises from the sea will then return like me
Because I am content to travel this road forever.
A grand tour in concentrate. Just add water.

(*you may have to pay extra for dolphins)

Driving the No 6 from Penzance to Mousehole and back became my main job for some five years and I can honestly say, I really enjoyed it. I get it that small buses aren't considered 'proper' buses within the bus-driving fraternity, but the regularity of the route gave me the chance to make lots of friends and having friends as passengers makes you a much nicer bus driver. The poem is nine minutes long when read, which is half the time it takes to make the bus journey. So, if you sat on the bus and read it really slowly, you could commentate on the journey...of course you might miss the dolphins!

YOU'RE LATE! (THE DRIVER'S RETURN)

An angry man, his face *Routemaster* red,
Gets on my bus and thrums like a diesel.
Swift to lay blame for my lateness, let's hope
He's prepared for my modest proposal.

"Ten minutes late and I want to know why!"
I say, "But won't this just take up more time?
As I'm known as the bus driver poet...
Pin back your ears and I'll tell you in rhyme."

You can't have it both ways...
You don't want us late.
You can't have it both ways...
You want us to wait.

Breakdowns or traffic congestion aside;
From which we drivers you must exculpate.
It's collective responsibility
That means it's your fault – the public – I'm late!

You stand there before me guilty as charged,
But I'm not saying it's your fault alone.
Here follows a list of transgressions which –
If you're innocent then cast the first stone

You can't have it both ways...
You want us to wait.
You can't have it both ways...
You don't want us late.

Some ask if I will wait while they're seated,
Then stand and chat to an old friend of theirs.
Others mutter that you're ten minutes late
Then add on two more by struggling upstairs.
(and back down)

Some stand with one foot placed on the platform;
Their pleading look is sweeter than violets.
Those already aboard inconvenienced
As we wait for their spouse in the toilets.

You can't have it both ways…
You don't want us late.
You can't have it both ways…
You want us to wait.

Some who just want to ask us a question
On tickets, destinations…even meals.
We do try our best as custodians
Of this information kiosk on wheels.

Some who choose to flag a passing bus down
To ascertain when the next one is due.
Exiting those lay-bys often takes time,
"Me let a bus out, you're joking aren't you?"

You can't have it both ways…
You want us to wait.
You can't have it both ways…
You don't want us late.

Some who are just not paying attention;
Lost in the Medusa gaze of their phone.
Come windmilling out at my passing bus...
I stop, they catch up...that's more minutes blown!

Some turn up as you're about to set off,
"That was good timing!" they say with a smile.
'Not for me', I muse, as they search their bags
And those lost seconds tick by all the while.

You can't have it both ways...
You don't want us late.
You can't have it both ways...
You want us to wait.

Some who've been patiently stood waiting then
Decide to rummage through bags when they
board.
Some drunk, unable to find their return;
I wait as all avenues are explored.

Some try stalling for time in the hope that
Their free concession will come into play.
Thereby holding up those concessionees;
Folk who were perfectly willing to pay.

You can't have it both ways...
You want us to wait.
You can't have it both ways...
You don't want us late.

Doubtless at some point you've been culpable
And if not, then I'm Oliver Hardy.
You see all these minutes accumulate
And end up making buses so tardy.

Now I've no problem with all the above
Whereas you, as your demeanour infers,
Clearly can't conceive why buses run late.
You'd be surprised how often it occurs.

You can't have it both ways…
You don't want us late.
You can't have it both ways…
You want us to wait.

As for the thought that we don't give a toss;
Drivers hate tardiness more than you'd know.
A driver who's late has let down his mate;
For there's no bus when it's their turn to go.

The way that I see it – people don't mind
Our being late if it suits their purpose
For those that do, on behalf of us all
I present you with this magnum opus.

You can't have it both ways…
You want us to wait.
You can't have it both ways…
You don't want us late.

I remember a man much like you, sir;
Who on arriving late at the station,
Made a stand before an exiting bus
In a Tianmen Square re-creation.

For his safety's sake that man was removed
The bus was now ten minutes overdue.
What did he care for those at the next stop?
The reason I ask is – that man was you.

You can't have it both ways…
You don't want us late.
You can't have it both ways…
You want us to wait.

It's the driver's job to balance these hopes;
To keep smiles on his passengers' faces.
But you play your part and he can smile too
And it might get you quicker to places.

So think on the next time I turn up late
I might just need you to play to your best
In helping me get my bus back on time
And my nerve endings a little less stressed.

You can't have it both ways…
You want us to wait.
You can't have it both ways…
You don't want us late.

Apart from traffic issues, the main reason buses run late is down to passengers. There, I've said it! Bus drivers hate being late because they miss out on their breaks or are late finishing. This poem was written for my colleagues.

I'M IN LOVE WITH THE B3306

(or *As I was travelling to St Ives; a metalled way took me by surprise.*)

I've fallen in love with a B road.
If I've shocked you, that wasn't my aim
But her curves drive me to distraction
And B3306 is her name.

My friends, they can't see the attraction…
"Isn't a road just old, plain and grey?"
"We've heard it said that she gets around…
So just use her to reach B from A."

True there maybe lines on her face and
The best part of her's over the hill.
My friends, you don't see her like I do
And I don't think that you ever will.

Yes, at times, she's far from her best; like…
At night when her danger's apparent
Or at dawn when she's moody in mist…
I turn a blind eye when she's errant.

Some warn me of her deviations…
"You won't like her when she starts to stray"
"Just like all roads; she'll leave you to roam"
Then I'll stay with her all of the way

To me she's a glamorous screen star
Who has seen it all back in the day.
I love her this Marilyn main road;
She's a jewel of a carriageway

When asked why it is she's so gorgeous
Says "Be seen in all the right places";
"A blue sky's as good as an airbrush:
"Accessories zhuzh-up plain faces"

Red campion and corn marigold
Adorn her peripheral tresses;
With primrose, foxglove and bluebell prints
Stella Mac would envy her dresses.

Her soundtrack of birdsong reminds me
Of a nocturne by Frederic Chopin.
Grasshoppers whirr with vigour for her
Like a passing air-cooled campervan.

Oh…let me be called to her bower;
Enough Eden to make Adam blush.
Where wind-tossed scents waft in soft verges
In an embrace so verdant and lush.

Given chance to lay in that boudoir;
I'd smooth out her grand corniche edges.
For true love's course takes curvaceous form
Despite what Will Shakespeare alleges.

I've seen her on *Facebook* with others;
Their photos and selfies above her.
Will such flirtations ever be thus,
My open-topped succubus lover?

I'll still be there for her in winter
When the coaches and tourists depart.
As she pulls back on that plain housecoat,
There'll be no rivals left for her heart

My love will be constant and true to
Her every gradient and camber;
Growing green shoots like a red, red rose
Yet steadfast forever in amber.

Not just fleeting, like visiting popes;
From me there'll be no tarmac kisses.
I'm proud I'm in love with a B road –
Don't tell the A30…my Mrs.

Of all the roads, I have driven on this is my
favourite. In the summer months, the traffic can be
a cross to bear, but the wonderful scenery more
than makes up for it. When all the Cornish hedges
are replete with Ragged Robin, Bluebells, Corn
Marigolds, Foxgloves…even Fuchsia and the cab
window is inches away from them. The scents and
sounds of the hedgerows are amazing. A truly
beautiful road that one can easily fall in love with.

31

LOVE ON THE ATLANTIC COASTER

Driving my bus down Alexandra Road
My heart missed a beat when I saw you there.
Stood at the stop, just like you said you would;
Half-remembered talk from a comfy chair.

I'm so glad you came; it brightened my day.
You, to see Sennen in all its glory;
Me, showing off as I drive my big bus;
Both playing parts in our own love story.

The Cove wasn't all that, due to the tide;
I was distracted by badly parked vans.
As we climbed up the hill, I reflected
How life dismantles the best of made plans.

But at Lands End you ascended as if…
From Heaven, cradling a small flask of tea;
Which, being tea in a flask, tasted yuk,
But you (and digestives) made it for me.

Love isn't about great big Valentines,
It's not about chocolates and flowers.
It's missing each other when you're apart
And passing time while you count down the
hours.

It's being together, loving, laughing
Even learning a Cornish paradigm;
Making the most of life with your partner.
For that is what love is all of the time.

One spring evening, I was telling Wendy, my wife,
how amazing it had been to see the waves at
Sennen Cove. I mentioned that I was doing the
same trip the following day and from the comfort of
her armchair, she said, "I might come with you,
tomorrow." I left it at that but was delighted when I
saw her standing at the bus stop the next day.

THE OMNIBUS COMPLEX

I love to see a preserved bus, the care
And affection imbued in her appearance
Suggests another time, an age
When mechanics filled the garage
And buses never broke down.
Washed and properly cleaned every night;
A time when standards were met.
A better time in many ways.
Yes, Jack and Reg were sexist
But they've gone now...haven't they?

So, I chose one, not just at random but,
Aided by memory to be the object of my desire.
BHG 756 No 37, a singleton, recalling
Journeys to the public baths from school;
The only joy for a nervous non-swimmer
Was the ride on her shiny, hard, red leather seats
Stitched tight and ribbed for less pleasure;
Climaxed by the packet of *Morning Coffee*
biscuits,
Devoured with chlorine-smelling fingers left
A happier child on his way back to school.

But I see her now...resplendent
And looking so good for her age;
Her rich rose madder skirt, sets her off
Against that pale cream decolletage.
Rose Madder and biscuit. Was there ever

A more beautiful name for the colour of a bus?
Kept apart by a piping of orange;
Sweet as a *Jaffa Cake* and just as more-ish.
Her orange-fired arrow indicators try
To distract your mind away from
The sensuous curves of her bustle
Where two huge TV screens windows
Are set in a custard-creamy console.
Beauty in the back end of a bus.

Born when curves were in vogue,
Before cigarettes came in flip-top packets;
But what lies under your flip top cowling?
"Many a good tune played on her engine, I bet!"
(I thought you said Jack and Reg were gone)
"I'm a Tiger, I'm a Ti-ger...I'm a Tiger, I'm a Ti-
ger!"
She roars...purring perfection.
A preserved purity – spotless.
Lovingly polished as part of her beauty regime;
Black mudguards keep the grime at bay
And that recognisable radiator
Her token concession to straight lines.
A Lancashire lass (nee Leyland), then married
To an East Lancashire coachbuilder.

Let's not talk of your cosmetic surgery;
Forced upon you for economic reasons.
A front entrance made you less
High maintenance...more commercially viable.
It was for me the initium of the terminus,

The point when business outmuscled service.
Thankfully you are preserved
And it's lovely to see you again
In the buff, devoid of garish marketing.
Be what you are, bus not billboard.

Once more, bidden by the memory's arousal,
Recall stirs into life, as your destination blind
Rolls through the endless possibilities for a young
boy…
Marsden Park Circular, Valley Mills, Reedley
Halt…
Further afield… Barley… where even was
Slaidburn?
As the stationary buses snoozed like sated kittens
Around the asbestos and glass of Nelson's
Market Hall;
The welcoming smell of *Horlicks*, meat pie and
gravy
Gusting out each time the market's double doors
open
Leave me bathed in that evocative aroma of days
gone.

Staring at her perfection, I sidle up to her,
Admiring her brooch, a family heirloom that
celebrates
Burnley, Colne and Nelson Joint Transport;
Three coats of arms belted and buckled into
place;

Alphabetically, not geographically in municipal
splendour.
A glowing tribute to those signwriters who were
both
Artisan and aesthete; old masters of their craft,
That of oil-based coach-painting and sign-writing
With the practised toil of the brush
Against the composure of the mahl stick.

Look at her...stunning in her voluptuousness!
She remains a work of art in my mind;
A Motor Lisa, a Venus di milometer.
Beauty...as well as beast.

Another love poem, this time for a preserved bus.
I do like a preserved bus, especially the ones from
my youth.

The Oily Cart Opera Company presents…
from Lightfoot & Sullivan's

THE BUS DRIVERS OF PENZANCE

THE *MODERN* CORNISH* BUS DRIVERS SONG

I am the very model of a modern Cornish bus driver;
Who drives our narrow lanes at the behest of ev'ry sightseer
And twitchers, cliffpath walkers and those searching for an ancestor,
For whom its very often free and funded by the taxpayer.
I'm very well acquainted with our towns and all their eateries;
With many cheerful facts about their shops and local galleries.
I'm happy to advise you on how best to plan itineraries
And help you with your shopping when you're coming back from Sainsbury's.

I'm very good and patient with those visitors from far away
Who need *ein wenig hilfe* with the language on their holiday;

A fun part of the job and I enjoy the social interplay
Of my communicating with those *qui ne parlent pas anglais.*
I know we're 'in the sticks' but I'm a modern bus professional.
Our journeys are much shorter than those made by Express National.
But I've to deal with numbers that are sometimes quite phenomenal
Because nowadays in Cornwall, our work is far from seasonal.

As doyen of the highway, let me be the one to ascertain
That I am blest with expertise in handling of the worst terrain.
A measured calm is needed to negotiate each narrow lane;
In short, I am perceived to be the master of my own domain.
When faced with granite walls I'm well aware of our fragility
And confident to handl'it to the best of my ability.
The tourists form a queue to shake my hand with regularity
And drivers from 'upcountry' are amazed by my temerity.

In getting you the best of fares, I'm more than economical.
On following the Highway Code, I'm almost evangelical.
I care for ev'rybody irrespective of their vehicle;
I'll even smile and wave my hand to people on a bicycle.
When faced with handling crises, I am armed with all that's requisite.
My language may be choice but rest assured its always apposite.
My comfort breaks are few and can be sorted with a quick visit
And think on if the bus breaks down, it's not my fault at all, is it?

In matters engineering, I confess to knowing bugger all.
In local knowledge, I excel and score quite high in general
With information animal, vegetable and mineral.
I hope I kept you smiling by performing all this doggerel.
So, whether you're a local or a less than frequent rider.
Feel free to place a medal on this great transport provider.
There is nothing I can't cope with (well except a Scottish fiver).
I am the very model of a modern Cornish bus driver.

This poem/song is a tribute to all my colleagues who do all of the above when driving around the challenging lanes of West Cornwall. Dear of 'em!

for the purpose of this poem and to appease the bus drivers who were actually born in Cornwall, 'Cornish bus driver' mean someone who is driving a bus in Cornwall.

41

JAM FIRST
(THE CREAM STAYS ON TOP)

If you've missed it on your media feed,
You may be wondering what the fuss is;
But a crowd's coming down from 'up country'
To take on the cream of Cornish buses.

They're promising new bells and whistles so
You may think that it's manna from heaven
But we brought you new buses and ticket
machines
And best of all we don't come from Devon.

They're being a bit disingenuous,
By saying they're bringing the prices down
As that's a government initiative
Which has to happen in each Cornish town.

Plymouth Citybus – now called *Go Cornwall*
Trying to make out that they're the bee's knees
When all of us know they can't get it right
With something simple like serving cream teas.

So, think on because it's important,
When that Devon bus pulls up at your stop.
Do you really want your transport run
By a company who puts jam on top?

This was just a bit of fun when our rival company, *Go Cornwall* (really the Devon company *Plymouth City Bus*) muscled in on the territory of *First Kernow*. Us drivers are good mates really...we never know when we are going to have to work for the opposition.

THE BRAIN FREEZE OF CHOICE
(JELBERT'S ICE CREAM)

The sigh of relief at winter's end
Is a given in temperate climes.
As we keenly count the harbingers –
Ones that signify sunnier times.

The confirmation that winter's done
Is a story the flowers foretell;
But long before the May Horns are blown
There's one marker we all know so well.

No cuckoo this with its trademark song,
No rhododendrons peerless display,
No bluebell swathe or gambolling lambs –
It's not a pastoral scene per se.

If nightingales sang in Regent Square
My heart couldn't feel any gladder.
Jelbert's ice cream shop is open but
It's harder to spot than an adder.

The shop itself does its best to hide;
Pays no homage to bygone summers
Or decks itself out in candy stripes;
It sort of resembles…a plumber's…

So, if tourists can't find it, well tough!
Less for them means it leaves us with more.
The only thing that we can't disguise
Is the queue coming out of the door.

And what of the product itself then?
Essentially vanilla ice cream.
Which seems to be doing quite nicely
Without need of a marketing team.

Ad men from Madison Avenue
Would dive frothing from their glassy towers;
Perplexed by *Jelbert's* achievements
Without need of their well-paid man hours.

No expense is spent on the signage –
Low overheads reflect in the price.
A steady hand with a black marker
On re-cycled cardboard will suffice.

No adverts…no website…no *Facebook*
A nod's as good as a wink, nudge, nudge.
Everything's left to word of mouth
And the mouth is the ultimate judge.

No choice other than how much you want.
It's the only decision to make.
Yes you can add the odd extra
Like a dollop of cream or a flake.

It's a lesson in understatement
Constant as the firmament twinkles.
The burden of choice removed for all
They don't even offer you sprinkles.

Let me take you to another place
Where every flavour is at hand.
You've got the freedom of choice you're craving
But indecisiveness takes command.

Your mind does its best to decide from
The multiple flavours of ices.
The upshot is that you find yourself
In a state of choice paralysis.

You're Buridan's hungry donkey placed
Equally between two bales of grass.
Starved because you can't make up your mind.
How could a donkey be such an ass?

Maybe that Henry Ford knew something
When he produced those first *Model Ts*.
Any colour…just as long as it's black;
The world's not ready for novelties.

So, when at last you've made up your mind
And plumped for the Chocolate Brownie;
The doubts creep in about Mint Choc Chip
Or the Orange and Marscapone.

Then you get a lick off someone else
And wish that was the one you'd chosen.
So, 'conceal, don't feel, don't let them know'
'Let it go!' like Elsa in *Frozen*.

You're pistachio green with envy
As you ogle someone's Eton Mess.
How could provision of such a range
Leave you feeling in need of redress?

You were given choice and you blew it
To pick the best was clearly your aim.
If failure is of your own making
Then you have nobody else to blame.

To maximise our experience
We research and review to excess
But expectations are so built up
Indifference rules nonetheless.

It seems it was all so much better
Before our world was categorised.
We still had the opportunity
To find ourselves pleasantly surprised.

Let's all embrace spontaneity
It may give cause for celebration
Perhaps the secret to happiness
Is to lower our expectations.

So, when tourists spy a queue that snakes
Out from an unremarkable shop...
Curiosity piqued, so much so
That it brings them to an unplanned stop

"This must be something special" they say,
"What on earth could be the attraction?"
They're in, they're out; no need to do more
Than complete a simple transaction.

Re-tasting their childhood memories
They bask in that glow of nostalgia.
Where the only downside might just be
That ice cream brain freeze neuralgia.

Hooray for the wonder of *Jelbert's*!
Cornwall's finest ice cream, I would bet.
No-one goes away disappointed.
Their expectations have all been met.

But for me their secret of success
Comes from NOT producing more lines.
Imagine how long that queue would be
If we all had to make up our minds.

Thursday 24th March 2016, I was driving one of the little buses from Mousehole to Penzance and there was a queue waiting for me at the stop at Newlyn Bridge. It was a pleasant day but people got on the bus with things on their minds like any other day. As I set off to leave, I noticed that *Jelbert's* Ice Cream shop had opened for business (it closes for the winter months) and already there was a queue forming outside. "Yay! *Jelbert's* is open!" I shouted and the passengers (with the exception of a few tourists who wondered what was going on) all forgot what they were thinking about and cheered along with me. That was it...the end of winter!

BUS LAY-BY BLUES

We all hate the bus not arriving on time
But no-one seems to mind they're making us late;
Calling us into a lay-by, then watching
As we wait for the traffic queue to abate.

Because nobody wants the back of a bus
To be all they can see from inside their car;
Slowing them down and choking with fumes 'til
they're
Blue in the face like someone from *Avatar*.

I mean, just how hard is it to shake your head
Or to wave your hand in a side-to-side way?
Much better than flapping your hands up and
down
When I pass by and spoil your plans for the day.

I'll be delighted if you choose to shun me;
By all means turn your back as I get nearer.
I'll simply raise my hand in celebration
In much the same way as that Alan Shearer.

As for those of you glued to your mobile phone,
Wrapped up in your *Facebook*, *Insta* and *Twitter*.
I pull in at the stop...you just look away
And you wonder why it is I feel bitter?

Then there's those who should have gone to *Specsavers*,
The ones who can't see the bus destination;
Still wearing glasses prescribed in the Eighties,
Call me in and make me late for the station.

But worst of the lot are those who flag you down
Then proceed to ask about some other bus.
"How would I know? I've been driving this one round!"
Yes, you might have thought it would be obvious.

Or one time I was stopped by a chap who asked...
If there was a *B & Q* in Penzance?
"Let's see...P...E...N...Z...A...N...C...E...no!"
I shut the doors - gone, without a backward glance.

So as soon as you're sure that I'm not for you
Then, please, just shake your head or wave us on through
Because it's not rocket science, after all,
It's not even Bus Driving NVQ 2.

Of course, I can't always blame the passengers.
I often stop for that little old lady
Dressed in her bright red coat, hat and black trousers
...only to find she's a Royal Mail post box...

When I said that passengers are one of the main reasons buses run late, well the performances I sometimes witness at bus stops play a big part in this. Calling the bus into the stop (especially if it is a lay-by) can lead to minutes being knocked off the timings, because nobody wants a bus to be driving in front of them, so getting out from that lay-by can be a real problem.

PENZANCE – EVIDENTLY PIRATE TOWN

Pirates in *Poundland*, Arrr-gos and *Boots*
Pirates in *Lloyds* and all the towns' banks
Pirates in *Burtons* ordering suits
Pirates in *Jewsons* ordering planks
They'll make you walk them and watch you drown
'Tis evidently Pirate Town

Pirates who know just what they're doing
Pirates in an abstemious state
Pirates in the post office queueing
Pirates after a fav'rable rate
At point two six doubloons to the pound
'Tis evidently Pirate Town

Pirates plundering char-i-dee shops
Pirates treasure is there to be found
Pirates partake in stylish teashops
Pirates dunking a ship's biscuit down
Whether it's 'scone', 'sconn' or maybe 'scown'
'Tis evidently Pirate Town

Pirates dress up in velvet and lace
Pirates in make-up, mascara'd eyes
Pirates who're more 'on' than 'in your face'
Pirates rememb'ring to moisturise
Doing your nails in your dressing gown
'Tis evidently Pirate Town

Pirates with beards of varying hue
Pirates, corsairs with very coarse hair
Pirates with dreadlocks, bumfluff boys too
Pirates fresh from the Barber-y chair
Fashions come around and go around
'Tis evidently Pirate Town

Pirates on mobility scooters
Pirates all eager to pimp their ride
Pirates sailing dangerous waters
Pirates prepare to come alongside
Be wary of toes when they run aground
'Tis evidently Pirate Town

Pirates pouring out of the station
Pirates incoming from all points east
Pirates dry, in search of libation
Pirates hungry, in search of a feast
There's a parrot in the lost and found!
'Tis evidently Pirate Town

Pirates board buses armed to the teeth
Pirates pressed and rammed to the gunwales
Pirates pre-loaded, needing to pee
Pirates cross-legged…short of urinals
The gutters run a goldeny-brown
'Tis evidently Pirate Town

Pirates hoisting the skull and crossbones
Pirates signal like pirates in books
Pirates parlaying with mobile phones
Pirates are texting, using their hooks
Less like semaphore, more sensurround
'Tis evidently Pirate Town

Pirates curse. They're givers not takers
Pirates use language. Pardon their French
Pirates oaths are not made by Quakers
Pirates expletives make dockers blench
More fecking swearing than Mrs Brown
'Tis evidently Pirate Town

Pirates acting like Neanderthals
Pirates deluded – think they're God's gift
Pirates molested by action girls
Pirates naked in the Wharfside Lift
Now it won't go either up or down
'Tis evidently Pirate Town

Pirates in Transit back home from France
Pirates loaded with baccy and rum
Pirates booty to sell in Penzance
Pirates tap noses. Pirates keep schtum
There are smugglers tunnels underground
'Tis evidently Pirate Town

Pirates with kids head to the seaside
Pirates who *are* kids head for the port
Pirates mess about on the quayside
Pirates are hoping not to get caught
The Scillonian's Tortuga-bound
'Tis evidently Pirate Town

Pirates emboldened, wild and raucous
Pirates can't hold back inhibition
Pirates fazed and losing their focus
Pirates head for the Seaman's Mission
There's mention of Press-Gangs in The Crown
'Tis evidently Pirate Town

Pirates dance to a frantic shanty
Pirates a-wooing ship's figureheads
Pirates strip off and do The Full Monty
Pirates in Penzance far from their beds
There'll be some rare sights around sundown
'Tis evidently Pirate Town
In Geneva, Humphry's spinning round
'Tis evidently Pirate Town.

There was a *Pirates on the Prom* event in 2014 when Penzance took the *Guinness* world record for having the most pirates in one place. Well, the record was lost to Hastings a year later so Penzance had another crack at it in 2016 (over 16,000 but we failed by 77 people). To see a town where everyone is dressed as a pirate is an amazing experience. This poem is a recollection of what I witnessed. The last line refers to Sir Humphry Davy, the scientist, inventor, poet and son of Penzance whose statue overlooks the main street of the town. He is buried in Geneva.

57

ON THE NAMING OF CORNISH COTTAGES

There is a house in Newlyn...
That I used to call my home.
It was called *Pendennis*...
Named after the castle I suspect.
Pendennis...a fine Cornish name
That means castle on the headland.
This *Pendennis* was at sea level;
Not really authentic, I felt
But then having lived in one of four
Modern semi-detached houses called...
Buccaneer Cottages...it could be worse.

Pendennis...
Its name was marked out
And hammered into the granite door frame
In those little black lead letters
That you see on Cornish gravestones.
Those letters that sometimes fall off...
Pendennis.

I was always worried that some of the letters
Of *Pendennis* would fall off
And me, not being skilled enough to replace them
(despite calling myself a wordsmith),
I would have to live in a house no longer called
Pendennis...
but...

Dennis...
(Why...what were you thinking of?)

Then I remembered in Mousehole...
There's a cottage that is called *Nigel*...
Just *Nigel*...and I got to thinking
That maybe *Nigel* meant something
Something I didn't know...Latin perhaps
But no...it is just a male name, Gaelic in origin
Just *Nigel*...

Isn't that what we do now...
Anthropomorphise everything?
Who calls their dog Rover or Gyp these days?
It's more likely to be Rosie and Jim.
Who calls their cat Fluffy or Tiddles now?
It's more likely to be Florence and Tim.
So why not with a cottage?
Imagine calling your home...
Trevor...

But in Carbis Bay, there is a house
Called *Trevor*...
Maybe it's Tre-Vor. Maybe it's Cornish
And means something else entirely.
But it looks like Trevor...and I sort of like that.

Giving your home a Cornish name
Lends it an air of authenticity...
A feeling of establishment.
New House becomes Chy Newydd

Sea View becomes Gwel-an-Mor
As a rule Cornish house names are a good thing
You're in Cornwall...embrace it.
Unlike those people
Who like to stake a claim for their homeland
Conquerors taking up the conqueror's position
Or missionaries...taking up the mission...
Well maybe not missionaries.
Whether it's Surbiton Cottage or Goodison Park,
Their home is a circle of covered wagons
Holding fast against the natives.
A little piece of Cornwall
That is forever England
...Or maybe Spain
Why move to Cornwall...
And call your house Torremolinos?

I've always been fascinated by words, as a child I would read everything. Sitting in the bath, I would read the back of the *Head & Shoulders* bottle, so much so that I now know what 'dandruff' is in six different languages. Stuck in roadworks at the top of a hill, I started reading the names of the cottages opposite. One was called *Riverside Cottage* and I got to thinking that there wasn't a river anywhere near…we were at the top of a hill and the nearest river was well over a mile away! Why would you call your cottage *Riverside*? Another cottage, one of a pair was called *The Cottage*…but the one next door wasn't called 'The Other Cottage'. It would be if I lived in it!

THE MERRY MAIDENS

Stood here since time immemorial;
Nineteen stones in perfect formation.
Not knowing why they were put here
Leaves it open to interpretation.

Calendar, congress or cenotaph?
And I do wish to labour the point;
That they were here a long time before
Christ had mastered his first dovetail joint.

Imagine times past, a parish priest,
The Whit Sunday walk to Lamorna.
A girl asks about the standing stones;
He seizes the chance to forewarn her,

"Of heedless young maidens who wanted
To dance on the holiest of days.
The Lord in his ire, turned them to stone;
Once wilful…they're now set in their ways."

"That's harsh…just for dancing" said the girl.
The priest had to strengthen his purpose.
"See those two other stones…there and there.
Well…that's all that's left of their pipers."

The girl's eyes widened and then narrowed;
A smart girl, not easily smitten.
"Why are they all in different fields?"
The priest said, "Because it is written."

The party processed down the valley
But the priest turned to Boskenna Cross
And prayed to his Good Lord for guidance
In enlight'ning his people who's boss.

Inspired by what happened to Lot's wife;
Paradigm of the Lord's will defied.
Turned from pillar of society
Into one of sodium chloride.

Thus, so inspired, he marched to the cove
And preached to his flock a fine sermon.
How failure to observe the Sabbath
Could turn people into...a dolmen.

He told how the girls danced regardless;
It was almost the new Sabbath day.
On hearing that first chime of midnight
The pipers thought they best get away.

The maids, so wrapped up in their dancing
Were just slaves to the rhythm and pace.
God decided to punish them by
Firmly keeping them all in their place.

The girl still had questions unanswered
But knew not to challenge her 'betters'.
The priest knew his tale was not binding
Until it was marked out in letters.

Once the tale's written and set in stone
It favours the writer's agenda.
Be it fable, Bible, *Daily Mail*...
Manipulative propaganda?

It seems that God's mercy or fury,
At least as far as I can perceive,
Depends on who's telling the story
And what control they wish to achieve.

God only appears unforgiving
In places like Islamic Asia
Where evil medieval thinking has
A will to apply certain pressure.

Which brings us back to that Cornish priest
And the power he needed to wield
That left us with petrified burkhas;
Ne-ne-nineteen of them in a field.

Stifling free will before it can breathe;
Imposition of his church's stance;
Our priest was just squaring the circle
To stop maidens from wanting to dance.

So why is God no longer angry
And showing a certain forbearance?
Why aren't we all turned flesh into stone
For failing our Sunday Observance?

No sandstones stand swearing in bunkers
On golf courses all over the land;
No milestones sit in just-polished cars
In lay-bys with a thermos to hand;

And why aren't there 70,000
Basalt columns supporting their team
The eleven menhirs of Man U
At Old Trafford's Theatre of Dreams?

No Granite stacks shelves at Sainsburys;
And no Serpentines service the tills.
The Millstone-Gritts don't meet the Flintstones
While out walking in the Malvern Hills?

Are megaliths spending megabucks
In a search of thrills and adventure?
Does Stonehenge see its sarsens ringed by
Smaller ones impressed by their stature?

Of course, God had previous for smiting;
At Minions, Bodmin Moor it is said,
A despicable meanness took place
That killed Sunday League Hurling stone dead.

So, with dancers, pipers and hurlers
Turned to stone by God's act of revenge
It does sort of beg the question
What on earth were they doing at Stonehenge?

A circle of standing stones on a hill high above Lamorna, The Merry Maidens are easily visible from the top of the open-top bus when heading towards Penzance from Lands End. In nearby fields are two huge individual stones, which are thirteen and fifteen feet in height, that are known as The Pipers (supposedly playing the music that caused the maidens to dance). The story of them being turned to stone for dancing on a Sunday seems to suggest a vengeful God, but if the story is told merely to stop people dancing then they are using God as a threat. When performing this poem, I often quote Elbert Hubbard, a US writer and philosopher, who said, "What we call justice is only (a) man's idea of what he would do if he was God."

THE TOWN CENTRE LIZARD OF HELSTON

A monster walks the streets of this town
And no, I don't mean like Frankenstein's.
It's Helston's own Town Centre Lizard
And I know because I've seen the signs.

Now I don't profess to be expert
In the field of reptilian ways.
In fact even as a little boy
I missed out on that dinosaur phase.

My knowledge of reptiles is wanting
And like you I'm as much in the dark;
Not armpit deep in dinosaur shit
Like that Sam Neill in *Jurassic Park*.

This lizard must be something to see
To warrant such 'in your face' signage.
The need to forewarn at all suggests
A creature of sizeable tonnage.

Let's be honest – size matters greatly.
It would hardly be a scary 'un;
If the little blighter was contained
In a two-foot square vivarium.

So, it's big but we need to know more
Regarding the nature of this beast.
I'm no David Attenborough, that's true,
But there is one thing I know at least.

I'm often found driving through Helston;
That's apart from the small hours of night
And I've yet to see its scaly hide.
It's nocturnal. It doesn't do light.

But where does it go during the day;
Does it spend the hours roaming old mines?
There's got to be somewhere it slumbers
Or what would be the point of those signs.

Maybe it sleeps in the boating lake…
You see what I'm thinking…Black Lagoon;
Dragging the boat and pedalo lines
As it emerges into the gloom.

Let's hope its intentions are vegan;
There's money to be made, if I'm right.
The tourists will flock in their thousands
To see Helston's own monster each night.

They're gonna be gutted in Scotland.
To be honest they must have some gall.
They've been coining it in with Nessie
And no-one's ever seen her at all.

Assuming our cash cow is land-based;
Make it *Flambards'* latest sensation.
All the gorse it ever could eat in
Its own custom-built habitation.

68

All these ideas are pie in the sky
If old 'Helsie's' some kind of killer?
Times as they are; the last thing we need's
A B movie Cornish Godzilla.

Now hang on that's got me wondering…
It's all smoke and mirrors and not good.
It might just be that while we're asleep;
Helston's runnels are flowing with blood

Where are the CARNAGE ON COINAGEHALL
Or MENEAGE STREET MASSACRE headlines?
Is the local press in on this and…
If it's hushed up then why put up signs?

That's it! They're not there for direction
To aid the lost, bemused and weary.
It's public liability and
Another conspiracy theory.

It seems that on entering Helston;
They're legal disclaimers – a warning.
Street cleaners wait those meeting their fate
Whose remains are scraped up by morning.

So once more it's down to the Council
We've no other plausible answers
Unless there is some place called Lizard?
There is? Oh…what were the chances?

When I first started driving buses, I ventured through towns that were unfamiliar to me; Helston being one of them. On the bus route in from Falmouth, I was always amused by the three road signs on the edge of the town that said, 'Town Centre Lizard' indicating two separate destinations. My imagination ran away with me, I guess.

**PORTHCURNO...STOP...COMMUNICATION...
BREAKDOWN...STOP...**

Porthcurno...unblemished beach above which
Cliff-hewn Minack holds a dramatic pose;
Always mindful that the sea plays the fringe;
Everything can be upstaged, it knows.

The one-time world's communication hub
Has realised it's not so big an' all.
Telegraphy's dead...telephony rules
And it can't even get a sig-a-nal.

The beach at Porthcurno is beautiful, The Minack Theatre that stands above it is awe-inspiring. Porthcurno was once the hub for the world's telegraph system, as cables headed out under that beach and were transported all around the world by boat, linking the great cities of this planet. Today, it is nigh on impossible to get a mobile phone or GPS signal in this valley. The worry of a bus breaking down in Porthcurno is only alleviated by the phone box at the turning circle. However, the fact that you can't be picked up by GPS is a different matter!

THROUGH THE WINDOW OF A CORNISH BUS

Looking in his rear-view mirror, the bus driver muses
That no-one actually looks out of the windows these days,
Except mothers teaching young ones their first words.
The old folk chat to each other at 25 miles an hour;
They have made this journey so many times that
Nothing short of a car accident or a horse on the loose
Will draw their head from the quotidian vocal workout of gossip.
The rest, fixated on their phones ignore the transient scenery
Of passing clouds, sea views, country lanes and idyllic harbours.

The driver remembers how it was for him as a child
When he and his mother would catch the bus to go shopping.
Because of Mum's polio they always had to stay downstairs.
He would run up the aisle and climb into a seat by the window,
She would fill the space alongside him, making him feel secure.

Through the Cinemascope window he had learnt
his first words...
Esso, *Shell*, those shiny forecourt symbols he
recognised
From their jingled adverts on the black and white
television.
He always hoped for the funny conductor, with
the hearing aid,
Who would turn the handle on the big metal ticket
machine,
Spitting out the paper snake with a snappy
satisfying whirr.
The ticket would be held out to the sparkle-eyed
child
Only for it to be pulled away from his grasp at the
last moment;
The ritual played out again and again at the
giggling child's delight;
But such things always have to end and he
remembered
A disappointment in triumph, as he clutched the
spoils in his tiny fist.

As the window's landscape changed to more
verdant scenes
His mother would encourage him to look out for
grazing animals;
He'd crow with delight at the sight of cows, horses
and sheep.
On cold, dank days, the windows doubled as a
chalkboard

Where the condensation allowed him to draw cars and faces
Or to carefully write his name in the smoke-grey medium.
Wiping away, he'd be sad when there was nowhere left to write
And content himself watching raindrops race to the windowsill.

When he was older, he would go upstairs and peep.
Gazing into the unseen world of first floor windows
In the hope of seeing something (he never knew what).
It was better in the evenings when those rooms became aquaria
Lit from within, portraying the brilliance of wildlife on dark nights.

In the first aeons of adolescence and later as a young man
He would prize a nearside window to get a closer view
(the offside put you further away) of the 'fit' young girls
As they parade their summer looks along the pavement.
The shy young boy, feeling as close as he would ever get to them.

Having meandered the bus through the archive of
his youth
The driver dis-engages autopilot and slows to a
halt
For a man with an outstretched arm running
towards the stop
Time ticks as he fumbles through his bag for a
weekly ticket
Places it on the machine; beads of sweat exude
on his brow
And drop and track the valleys of his
weatherproof sleeve.
Darting eyes betray the stress already driving his
day
Hindered by his bag of worries, he sways up the
aisle of the bus,
Slumps in a seat and reaches for the only thing
that can help.
He swipes through the *CalmerU* app on his phone
Ignoring 'Mountain Stream', 'Garden Rain' and
'Sunlit Sea'
To the one that works best for him...
"A vision of passing clouds, sea views, country
lanes
And idyllic harbours"
He sighs...calmer now
It's called...
"*Through the Window of a Cornish Bus*"

As a bus driver in this wonderful land of Cornwall, I would glance back at my passengers and marvel at how many of them would miss the beauty of the land and seascape around them as they concentrated on their mobile phones. People have boarded buses at the bus station and failed to notice that they are travelling in completely the wrong direction because they have been fixated on their mobile phone. I recall one young woman who got as far as Newbridge (twenty minutes into the journey to St Just) before asking me when we would be getting to St Ives.

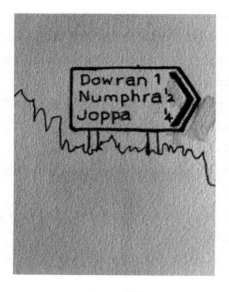

DRE FENESTER KYTTRYN IN KERNOW

(translated into Cornish by Nicholas Williams)

Hag ev ow meras i'n myrour wàr dhelergh, ma
drîvyor an bùss ow predery
Na vÿdh den vëth ow meras in mes a'n fenester
hedhyw i'n jëdh,
Ma's mammow yn unnyk ow tesky an kensa
geryow dh'aga flehes.
Yma an bobel goth ow kestalkya pymp mildir
warn ugans in eur;
Y re wrug an viaj-ma mar venowgh na wra
Tra vÿth ma's droglamm kerry pò margh dienkys
Tedna aga fedn dhyworth omassayans levow
scavel an gow.
Nyns usy an remnant, fastys dh'aga clapgùthow,
ow merkya an vuys ow passya,
Cloudys ow tremena, semlant an mor,
bownderyow keyn pow pò porthow pyctùresk.

Yma an drîvyor ow perthy coth a dhedhyow y
floholeth,

Pàn wre va ha'y vamm kemeres an kyttryn rag
mos dhe'n shoppys.
Awos pôlyô Mammyk res vedha dhodhans gortos
awoles.
Ev a vydna ponya an dremenva in bàn ha
crambla in esedhva ryb an fenester,
Hy a wre lenwel an spâss ryptho, hag ev a
omglôwa yn saw.
Der an fenester Cynemascôp ev a dheskys y
kensa geryow ...
Esso, *Shell*, arwedhyow munys an ragcortys o
aswonys dhodho
Dhyworth an argemynnow kenys wàr an
bellwolok dhu ha gwynn.
Ev a'n jeva govenek pùpprÿs a'n tôkynor coynt
esa darbar clôwes dhodho,
A vynna trailya an dornla wàr jyn brâs metol an
tokynnow
Ha trewa in mes an nader a baper in unn whyrny
yn teg.
Y fedha an tôkyn sensys in mes dhe'n flogh
splann y dhewlagas
May halla va bos tennys in kerdh dhyworto orth
an prÿjweyth dewetha;

79

Y fedha an devos gwaries arta hag arta ha sordya
folwharth an maw lowenek;
Saw res yw dhe daclow a'n par-na dewedha
pùpprÿs hag ev a remembras
Tùll in y vyctory, pàn wrella dalhena an pray in y
dhorn bian.

Dell esa an wolok dhyworth an fenester ow
chaunjya dhe vuys glassa,
Y vabm a wre y inia dhe whelas bestas ow pory;
Assa wre va cria gans joy ow qweles buhas,
mergh ha deves!
Dedhyow yêyn ha glëb, an fenestry a servya avell
astell galhen
May whre an glûth gasa dhodho tenna kerry tan
ha fâcys
Poken screfa y hanow gans rach i'n main
mogloos.
Pàn wrella ev deseha, y fedha trist na veu tyller
gesys rag screfa
Hag ev a omgontentya owth attendya an
glawlednow ow fysky dhe legh an fenester.

Pàn vedha ev cotha, ev a vydna mos in bàn ha
gîky.
Ow meras orth bÿs dywel fenestry kensa leur an
treven
In govenek a weles neb tra (ny wodhya ev
bythqweth pandra).
Gwell o gordhuwher pàn vedha chambours gwrës
pyskvaow
Golowhës wàr jy, ow tysqwedhes splander
goodhvêwnans i'n nos tewl.

In kensa osow y adolescens ha moy adhewedhes
avell den yonk
Ev a garsa fenester ryb tenewen an fordh may
halla dhe well gweles
(Te a via pelha in kerdh wàr an tu aral) an
mowysy yonk teg
Hag y ow kerdhes i'ga dyllas hâv an cauns ahës.
An maw yonk methek a omglôwa mar glos
dhodhans dell vedha nefra.

Warlergh gwil dhe'n bùss gwandra dre govyon y
yowynkneth

Yma an drîvyor ow dystaga an honenlewyor, ow
lent'he hag ow stoppya
Rag den, istynys y vregh, usy ow ponya tro ha'n
savla.
Yma an termyn ow tyckya ha'n den ow fysla der y
sagh rag tôkyn seythen,
Y settya wàr an jyn; yma pederow whës ow sevel
wàr y dâl
Hag ow codha hag ow sewya nansow y vrehel
stanch.
Ma gwibya y dhewlagas ow tyskevra an dennva
owth hùmbrank y jorna solabrës;
Sprallys der y fienasow, ym va ow lesca tremenva
an bùss in bàn,
Owth esedha yn idhyl, owth hedhes y dhorn rag
an unn dra a weres.
Yma va ow scubya der an dowlennyk *CalmerU*
wàr y glapgûth
Heb gwil vry a 'Gover Meneth', 'Glaw in Lowarth '
Na 'Howl wàr an Mor'
Erna dheu va bys onen a vydn y servya yn tâ
"Vesyon a'n cloudys ow tremena, semlant an
mor, bownderyow keyn pow
Ha porthow pyctùresk".

82

Yma va owth hanaja…hag ev moy hebask.

Y dhôwys yw henwys

"Dre Fenester Kyttryn in Kernow."

It was such a delight and an honour when I was asked by Nicholas Williams, one of the foremost experts on the Celtic languages in the world, whether he could translate my poem *Through the Window of a Cornish Bus* into Kernewek (the Cornish Language). I have placed it in this book, knowing full well that most of the people will skip past it as they don't understand the language, but I think it deserves a permanent place. I, myself, am learning the Cornish language because, despite what some might think, it is not a dead language. It lives on in the place names that I drove buses through over the last thirteen years. As soon as you come over the Tamar Bridge (just as you come over the Severn Bridge into Wales), the names of towns and villages become more and more different from those you left behind. Cornwall is another country.

THE LAST BUS
(…and Death shall have no Dominoes)

Underground now in a wooden box;
Instead of above in one of metal and glass.
The absence of a door of any kind
At least allows me to rest in peace.
That mantra of the bus driving fraternity
"An empty bus is a happy one",
May be wide of the mark in this case,
As I find myself incarcerated
In this receptacle for used tickets only.
Ignoring the small brass turning handle
That hangs above me like that Greek fellow's
sword;
I seek the periscope to look upstairs but
Its absence confirms what I already know –
My last vehicle is a single-decker.
Just me, my timetable and duty board;
The latter, in truth a laminated sheet of A4
That marks out my journey…
My final journey…
It is blank.

What was it brought me here?
One of those days…I'm late, I'm late
For everyone else's important date.
At the next stop a man in black,
One arm gauntleted in an aluminium crutch,

84

Looks somewhat theatrically at his watch.
He takes no notice of the time
As his dumb show is for my benefit;
Me the one who is in the thrall of
The large digital clock on my ticket machine.
He wants me to know that he knows I am late.
The great metal crutch scythes out into the road,
Arcing like a crusader's longsword
Into the fray…ready for conflict
(Clearly it requires substantially more
Than just an arm in this instance).
There with blade and timepiece, he clutches
In the white crab's-legged fingers of his hand,
His concessionary pass like a small shield…a
buckler.
I hate you longsword. I hate you buckler.

Drawbridge down, he mounts the bus
And draws up terms for my surrender.
"You… (not even a 'Sir' here) are late!"
As if I didn't know…the clock on the machine,
remember?
I tell him that I'm far from happy about it myself.
I'm late for me. My journey home
To wife and family will be (what's the
word?)…later.
He then wastes time (that oh so valuable
commodity)
By asking me why I'm late.
If I told him…I doubt his anger would allow him to
listen?

And so, it continues…
Late coming into the station,
The standing load all eager to alight
But slow to accomplish the deed.
For my next trip…my last journey
More angry faces line up in wait.
Ready to complain…ready to question
About return times…or just why
I'm late…leaving the station.
The knock-on effect actualises
The Law of Cumulative Lateness*…
"Once a bus is late, it can only become later still"
Those twenty minutes will not be made up
They will breed, incubated by fate
On a route that challenges the driver.
The single-track roads…press once
As headway is no longer maintained
As much as dismembered…press once.
The on-coming tractor and trailer
And the hundred-yard reverse…press once.
The driver out of his campervan comfort zone
The timid tourist puts a back wheel…press once
Halfway up a Cornish hedge and nods
In meek obeisance as I process by…press once.
I feel the vein in my temple throb
Protruding like a bell strip…press once.
It keeps ringing but no one gets off
The snickering kids upstairs…
Pressing more than the prescribed once.
Ask not for whom the bell tolls;
Isn't it obvious as I fight the early evening traffic?

Departing the beach at Porthcurno
Or the afternoon performance at the Minack
Theatre?
I push like some kind of matinee idol
Against a pouring tide of humanity;
Each car a canned concentrate
Of a laughing theatre audience
As I press on.

At the hairpin bend overlooking Treen village
He waits once more, this time in a black cloak
A hood cowling his imagined features.
Now the timepiece is made of glass and sand.
His scythe gleams with certainty
As it arcs out like a great metal crutch.
My time has come...Death waits for me
I am compelled to bring the bus to a halt;
Even though it is not an official request stop.
Opening the doors for the last time
I take comfort from the good book.
The Bus Driver's Manual on greeting a passenger
*I turn to face him and make eye contact to show I
am genuinely interested in what he is saying.*
"It is time" says Death.
*I make sure I listen carefully to what he is saying
and do my best to give a clear and concise
answer.*
"Fuck..." I say.
*I keep my facial expression friendly, open and
clear. Remembering to keep my hands away from*

my face when listening and responding using a
steady and moderate tone of voice.
"Any chance of a game of chess?"
"Do you even play?" says Death.
"How about a game of dominoes?"
He shakes his head.
"Those things only happen in films."
His final words…so much better than mine.
I am willing to smile readily if it is appropriate to
do so.
Remembering Bob Monkhouse's gag;
His wish to die like his father peacefully in his
sleep
Not screaming and terrified like his passengers.
The passengers who, as I fly over the hairpin's
edge
Will be meeting their own version of Death?
The passengers who will never reach The
Minack.
Not the monk's house, this mynach
But a stony place…a hard place
I look around for the rock.

Underground now in a wooden box
Reaching my destination blind
To what lies ahead…if anything.
I present my final waybill.
I'm the late bus driver
Having arrived at the terminus.
"Mortem omnibus nobi venit"
Which means "Death comes for us all"

By bus...I think.
I take hold of the brass handle overhead
And the letters on the stone six feet above
Turn through the various destinations
Birth
Childhood
Learning
Love
Family
Hope
Until they stop at...
Sorry I'm Not In Service.

*"The Law of Cumulative Lateness" comes from *The Maintenance of Headway*, one of the few novels about bus driving, by former London Transport bus driver, Magnus Mills. Of his many books, all of which I recommend, I recognise that *The Maintenance of Headway* is written primarily for bus drivers

This poem was born out of many things. The frustration of keeping a bus on time on a particular challenging route. The annoying habit of people looking at their watch when you arrive late at their stop (and people holding walking sticks aloft...which particularly riles bus drivers), we do know we are late...and we hate it more than you! Then there is Ingemar Bergman's film *The Seventh Seal*, where a wandering knight meets the personification of Death...and an idea I had for a deceased bus driver's headstone.

I'M NOT A PROPER POET, ME
(excerpt from a longer poem)

Back when Adam delved and Eve spun...who
then was Sir John Betjeman?

I'm not a proper poet, me.
It's all good fun, I guarantee.
Don't be put off on the say-so
Of some academia nuts.
See what I did there? (yeah you did)
And may I say that line took guts.
That's the point I'm trying to make,
Is be brave and not just clever.
Believe you can be a poet
With courage and some endeavour.
Buy a Rhyming Dictionary
Be surprised at where you're taken.
"Say what you see!" like on *Catchphrase;*
Stand up for the point you're making.
If you can reach out to people
Who think they don't like poetry...
That see it as nothing more than
A bowl of verbal pot-pourri.
If elitists lead you a dance
By calling it...terpsichory;
Be like Lowry, as smart as paint
And stick with your matchstickery.
Love John Cooper Clarke's "Midnight Shift"
As much as John Donne's "Break of Day".
The world is full of new readers

Who all bought *Fifty Shades of Gray*.
Which brings it back to me again
The ageing arthritic rapper...
Whose hip-op's on the NHS
And drug of choice is a cuppa.

Collaborating with JayZee?
I'm not a proper poet, me.

I'm not a proper poet, me.
Never taken seriously.
You see, I'm a punchline poet;
My poetry plays like a joke.
It drips with flipping flippancy
(It's annoying to certain folk).
I'm a poet with a purpose
And it's not just to make you laugh.
Like French statesman Jean-Paul Marat
I write most of it in the bath.
If poetry moves you to tears
Then why not move you to laughter?
I might not win the Nobel Prize,
It's not trophies that I'm after.
I'm not in it for the money;
I'm happy with any acclaim.
The only thing I ask of you
Is that you remember my name.

Gray Lightfoot...*First Bus* employee.
I'm not a proper poet, me.